The Public and the Police

The Public and the Police

Harriet Sergeant

Civitas: Institute for the Study of Civil Society
London
Registered Charity No. 1085494

First Published May 2008

© Civitas 2008
77 Great Peter Street
London SW1P 2EZ
Civitas is a registered charity (no. 1085494)
and a company limited by guarantee, registered in
England and Wales (no. 04023541)

email: books@civitas.org.uk

ISBN 978-1-903386-66-8
Independence: Civitas: Institute for the Study of Civil
Society is a registered educational charity (No.
1085494) and a company limited by guarantee (No.
04023541). Civitas is financed from a variety of private
sources to avoid over-reliance on any single or small
group of donors.

All publications are independently refereed. All the
Institute's publications seek to further its objective of
promoting the advancement of learning. The views
expressed are those of the authors, not of the Institute.

Typeset by
Civitas

Printed in Great Britain by
The Cromwell Press
Trowbridge, Wiltshire

Contents

Author

Harriet Sergeant is the author of *Welcome to the Asylum: immigration and asylum in the UK* (Centre for Policy Studies, 2001); *No System to Abuse: immigration and health care in the UK* (CPS, 2003); *Managing not to Manage: management in the NHS* (CPS, 2003); *Paying Twice: policing a local community* (Civitas Review, Vol. 1, issue 4, December 2004) and *Handle with Care: an investigation into the care system* (CPS, 2006). She has also written three books: *Between the Lines: Conversations in South Africa* describes the effect of apartheid on some of its Indian, coloured, black and Afrikaaner inhabitants in the early 1980s; *Shanghai* is a history of the world's most international city between 1927 and 1939; and *The Old Sow in the Back Room* recounts her experiences of Tokyo where she lived for seven years. She has written for numerous newspapers and magazines in Britain and abroad and frequently appears on radio and television.

Executive Summary

Expenditure on the police force is at record levels. In terms of numbers and budgets, it has never been so large. In spite of this there is widespread public dissatisfaction resulting in a steep increase in complaints against the police, with many coming from law-abiding, middle-class people who complain of rudeness and neglect of duty. It is hard to get the police to respond to reports of crime and anti-social behaviour. Investigations are lacklustre and often abandoned.

The police, in their turn, complain of being short of resources. Although police numbers in England and Wales are historically high, compared with other developed countries they are low. Furthermore, crime rates in England and Wales are amongst the highest in the developed world, so the workload of officers is unmanageably large. Officers have been submerged by a flood of paperwork, so that only 14 per cent of their time is spent on patrol. This paperwork is done at the expense of officers on the beat and responding to crimes.

The public have no power to influence policing. All decisions are taken by politicians and their appointees, but there is no accountability within the system. Since the Police Act 1964 successive governments have accrued power to the centre.

Centralisation has led to politicisation and the introduction of targets. Bonuses are paid to senior officers based on compliance with targets. In order to achieve the required level of detections, police officers pursue those who will yield easy convictions, such as speeding motorists or high-spirited students, rather than the serious and persistent offenders who are destroying the quality of life in communities. Officers are now classifying as crimes things that would previously have been dealt with informally or under a different classification. Targets affect the sort of work that police undertake: arresting a child for chalking on the pavement counts as a 'sanctioned detection', the painstaking work of tracking down a missing child does not. One officer said: 'We are bringing more and more people to justice—but they are the wrong people.'

The target the public would most like to see met is the absence of crime—the first of the Nine Principles of Policing laid down for the Metropolitan Police on their foundation in 1829. To this end, police officers need to be visible in their communities.

The decision to prosecute is taken by the Crown Prosecution Service, which has its own targets to achieve in terms of successful prosecutions. This makes the CPS unwilling to prosecute cases where they are not convinced the evidence is rock solid. This leads to many potential prosecutions being dropped, leaving the public feeling let down and allowing criminals to feel they have 'got away with it'. Prison overcrowding has created pressure for non-custodial sentences. Many criminals, including burglars, rapists and violent attackers, get no more than a caution. Often they continue to offend, and it becomes progressively more difficult for the police to catch them as they learn by their experience of the system.

Police officers swear an oath of allegiance to the Queen, not the Prime Minister. Unlike many other police forces, British police were not intended to be servants of the state, but of the communities they serve. Their powers are personal, used at their own discretion and derived from the crown. This essential feature of British policing—policing by consent—is now in jeopardy.

Methodology

This report looks at what is going wrong between the public and the police. It is based on interviews and research over six months between June and December 2007. I interviewed police from every level of the service: constables, sergeants, inspectors, chief super-intendents, borough commanders, deputy chief constables and retired members of the former Special Branch. I also sat in on a custody desk, patrolled with my local PCSOs, attended police conferences and local police forums and have been in and out of my local police station an embarrassing number of times. I was fortunate to have the co-operation of the Police Federation who arranged the majority of my interviews. Researchers for the Police Federation also provided me with transcripts of interviews from 14 different forces around the country. In order to preserve the anonymity of those interviewed, they have not been named. Nonetheless, I owe them a large debt of gratitude.

Abbreviations

ACPO	Association of Chief Police Officers
BCS	British Crime Survey
BCU	Basic Command Unit
CCJS	Centre for Crime and Justice Studies
CID	Criminal Investigation Department
CPS	Crown Prosecution Service
IPCC	Independent Police Complaints Commission
NFA	No further action
PACT	Partners and Communities Together
PCSO	Police Community Support Officer
PND	Penalty notice for disorder
Response	Those officers who are despatched to the scene of a reported incident

Introduction

Why Can't We Get the Policing We Want?

There is a huge gap between how we want to be policed, how the police want to police us and how we are actually policed. Why is there this gap and what can be done about it?

First of all, what does the public want? One sergeant put it simply. The public, he said, are not interested whether burglaries have gone up or down by five per cent. 'They want to know that when they go to bed at night that they ain't going to get broke into; when they get up in the morning the car is still going to be on the drive and their mums, dads and granddads can walk in the shop in the morning to get the paper and come back again without being robbed.'

What kind of policing the public is getting is clear from a recent letter to the *Daily Telegraph*. The writer had noticed eight police manning a number plate recognition post. Why, he wonders, do the police need eight men for this task? But when his house is burgled or there is a local affray, 'you cannot find a policeman for love nor money'[1]

The police force, like the NHS, is a formidable institution whose size and cost this government has increased dramatically over the last ten years. By 2011 spending on the police will have risen to £10 billion, two thirds of the law-and-order budget. Never has the police service had so much money, so many officers or such access to technology. Yet never have the public and the police been so dissatisfied. What has gone wrong?

Unlike the USA, the public here lacks the power to get the policing they want. Their local police force is not accountable. Neither they, their democratically elected local councillors nor their MP have any influence over the strategy of their local force, its funding or the appointment or removal of its Chief Constable. If the Chief Constable wants to close police stations against the wishes of the community, he can do so. If he wants his response teams to spend the day chasing tabby cats, there is little to stop him. A local Councillor from Kent dismissed the current system as 'cheating the people. They don't ask for much and what they do ask for isn't unreasonable.'[2]

Instead the 43 police forces in England and Wales are wholly accountable to the Home Office and the Secretary of State—'the Chief Constable of Chief Constables,' as one police officer put it. Since the Police Act 1964 successive governments have accrued power to the centre. It is the Home Secretary and not the local council who has the power to set police budgets, intervene in forces that fail to meet centrally determined performance indicators and punish Chief Constables with not only the sack but, most crucially of all, the loss of their pension. That is real power.

As in the NHS, centralisation has led inexorably to the politicisation of the force. Law and order is a hot political issue. The government cannot be seen to fail.

But with total control comes total responsibility. As with the NHS, increased investment equals tighter government control in the form of national targets, interference and the bureaucracy created by central intervention. Civil servants appear to believe that challenging targets results in change. But too many targets see the system falter. There are only so many on which an organisation can concentrate. When resources are limited there have to be trade offs. Whitehall appears not to understand this. When Chairman of the Audit Commission, James Strachan told the Select Committee on Public Administration of targets: 'There is a dire need to train people in how to set these targets.' Those responsible for setting targets at senior level suffer from: 'a lack of real world delivery experience and this is shown time and time again.'[3] He was talking about the NHS but his comments apply equally well to the police.

Each new initiative, however beneficial in theory, requires staff, time and funds to implement. As in the Department of Health, there is no requirement for civil servants in the Home Office to make that calculation. There is no attempt to see how the latest big idea plays out on an overstretched ward or beat.

Targets are not all bad. A well thought-out target forces public servants to look at what they do and how they do it. Unfortunately, as in the NHS, the government measures the wrong things and measures too much. Worse, it tolerates dodgy data for political ends. Bad targets coerce otherwise ethical public servants into unethical behaviour. Serious crime is ignored and

3

minor crime elevated to the level of the serious in order to satisfy the measurement regime. The police are forced to make fools of themselves. And for what end? Fulfilling government targets is not leading to better policing. On the contrary the police complain that they are criminalising a generation and alienating the public. One officer said: 'We are bringing more and more people to justice—but they are the wrong people.'

The police are one part of the criminal justice system which includes the Crown Prosecution Service and the courts. All three work to different targets in conflict with each other and, too often, with the victim's quest for justice. The desire of the police to prosecute, for example, can conflict with the CPS target of achieving successful prosecutions. The victim's sense of justice is at odds with government sentencing guidelines designed to lessen prison overcrowding. As the first point of contact, the police get the blame. 'I get fed up,' said one Chief Superintendent, 'with apologising to the public for the failures of the criminal justice system.'

Targets also miss the point of what the public wants. The Home Office judges each police force by how many crimes they detect and clear up. The public desire something different. They do not want the crimes happening in the first place. A poll asked members of the public to prioritise the activities they wished the police to spend time on. They placed preventing crime, community policing and foot patrol at the top of the list. These are all about the deterring effect of a visible, uniformed officer walking around the neighbourhood. On the other hand crime detection was placed second from bottom.[4]

The public see the foot patrol, top of the list and chosen by almost 60 per cent of those surveyed, as the basis of policing. It is a view that was shared by Sir Robert Peel, the founder of the police force and appears as one of the Nine Principles of Policing first published in 1829 and issued to every member of the Metropolitan Police. It states that 'the test of police efficiency' is 'the absence of crime and disorder.' It is not 'the visible evidence of police action in dealing with them.' (See Appendix, p. 79.)

Sadly the government prefers to reward that 'visible' evidence of police action. The absence of crime and disorder is not a target—not even for Safer Neighbourhood Policing. As one constable wrote on a Police Forum, 'I remember when it was a matter of pride to come back after a night shift to find no crimes had happened. Now all we are asked is why no one was locked up or issued a PND'. Another recalled wistfully: 'There was a time when you were actually measured on how quiet you managed to keep your patch'.

All interviews with the police were characterised by a high level of bitterness and frustration. Ill thought-out government policies are fast demoralising a group of professionals who are ready to die in the course of duty. Ten have lost their lives since the start of the new millennium. Despite recent headlines, no one mentioned pay. Central control and its corroding effect were the issues. In order to score politically, they believe the government has sacrificed their integrity, the integrity of the force and their relationship with the community. 'The police', said a superintendent, 'have become an extension of the government.' A retired deputy chief constable asserted: 'Politics currently control the police'.

Rank-and-file officers pointed out that on joining they had sworn an oath to serve the Queen—not the Prime Minister. Unlike many other forces, British police have never been servants of the state. Officers' powers are personal, used at their own discretion and derived from the crown. This essential feature of our policing is now in jeopardy.

Targets are also undermining a culture unique to a civilian institution with it emphasis on solidarity and hierarchy. Officers found themselves in competition with each other to achieve targets in an organisation where teamwork is paramount.

Many felt their senior officers had abandoned them and sold out to the Home Office. Most interviews were taken up with this complaint. Top officers receive bonuses ranging from £5,000 to £15,000. These bonuses depend on their men achieving targets set by the Home Office. One officer said: 'I love my job but I hate the way I am pressured to make others look good.' Other officers went further. They accused their superiors of turning the force upside down, undermining the ethos of policing and jeopardising relations with the public, 'all for two good holidays a year. Marvellous isn't it?'

It is not just the rank-and-file who share this view. When asked about the principle of constabulary independence if local councils were to control police funding, a Conservative MP pointed out that the Association of Chief Police Officers (ACPO) had already turned itself into 'a division of the Home Office'.[5] A retired member of Special Branch wondered where that left the force. 'What is the purpose of the police now? I would love to know.'

1

Why Has the Public Lost Faith in the Police?

That the public has lost faith is clear, 'despite', as one officer pointed out, 'all those good crime figures'. Police funding is up a quarter in real terms since 2001, making it the highest amongst the OECD countries. The UK spent 2.5 per cent of GDP on public order and safety in 2004, well ahead of the US, Spain, Germany and France.[1] Despite this largesse, by 2006 only 25 per cent of the public had any confidence in the government's ability to crack down on crime and violence — the lowest percentage out of the five countries and considerably below the next lowest: Spain with 40 per cent.[2]

This growing alienation between the public and police is a worrying development. The police, like the NHS, have exerted a powerful hold on the nation. Their fairness defines us. They represent a particular conception of English identity and social order. They have been able to call upon support from significant sections of the population not just because of what they do but because of what they represent.

In 2004 I did a survey of crime in my neighbourhood in West London.[3] To my neighbours, comfortably off, middle-class and traditional supporters of law and order, the police are part of the problem — not the solution. The police judge themselves by the numbers of arrests made. We judge the police by the absence of crime. It is a fundamental difference. The police were either not interested or unable to deal with low-level crime. Most importantly, they did not take it seriously.

A retired businessman and member of the Conservative party summed up the general view: 'The police don't regard petty crime as crime.' He reported his car stolen to the police. 'Bad luck', was their only response. One evening he saw three youths smash the window of a local shop and rip out the till. He called the police who turned up immediately and caught the boys. My neighbour offered to be a witness, 'not a light undertaking' as he remarked, but heard no more. The next time he saw five louts smash a telephone box, he just kept walking. He went on: 'The police's job is to identify crime, encourage people to report it and then keep them informed.' Their failure to do this is contributing to 'a massive lack of public confidence.'

American neighbours used to a more accountable police force expressed the most outrage. 'What is wrong with this institution?' demanded one after she failed to get any response to a case of petty thieving. On Christmas morning five cars in a row had their tyres slashed outside my front door. As we gathered together on the pavement, not one of us thought to call the police.

My neighbours are not alone. In the most recent British Crime Survey 50 per cent of respondents thought the police in their area did an excellent or good job. A 50 per cent satisfaction rate is a sorry result for any institution. Negative attitudes towards the police depend on personal experience: people who had no contact with their local police over the previous year were more likely to rate their force as doing an excellent or good job than those who had. People who had been victims of crime were even less likely to rate their local police as doing an excellent or good job than those had not been a victim.[4]

One of my neighbours described her experience. An attractive young mother, she was helping her 18-month-old son out of the car when she was set upon by three men. She was punched repeatedly in the throat while being robbed of jewellery. She passed out in front of her child. Initially the police reaction was good because of the level of brutality and because a child was involved. She was kept updated by a detective who then moved to the murder squad, and my neighbour heard no more. A policeman spent three hours taking her statement. The computer kept crashing. He told my neighbour he would finish it off then drop it round. Seven months later he rang and asked her to come in and sign it. 'I was really shocked. I thought he had done it long before.' A detective made an appointment then never turned up or rang to apologise. She said: 'Frankly it has been a very frustrating process and a total shambles.'

Complaints against the police have also risen. During 2006/07 a total of 29,637 people made complaints against the police in England and Wales. The annual total has doubled in the past three years and is now the highest in the 17 years since allegations were counted nationally. Traditionally it is young men who claim assault by officers—35 per cent of complaints were made by under-17-years-olds.[5] But this year a new pattern is emerging and a new kind of complainant.

The big increase is due to allegations from law-abiding, middle-class, middle-aged and retired people. They were upset by officers' rudeness and behaviour. Complaints about 'neglect or failure in duty' by officers accounted for 24 per cent of the total received, while 'incivility, impoliteness or intolerance' accounted for 21 per cent.

Nick Hardwick, the chairman of the Independent Police Complaints Commission (IPCC), pointed out that incivility and neglect of duty—'what are sometimes perceived as relatively minor matters'— make up almost half of all allegations against the police. The complaints reflect my neighbours concerns: 'rudeness, not keeping someone informed about a case as promised and failing to investigate someone's crime properly.' He points out that for the law-abiding citizen 'their contact with the police, whether real or perceived, can have a profound impact on their confidence in the police service as a whole'.[6] The loss of public confidence is a serious matter. The police cannot police without the backing of society. Without trust and consensus it is very difficult and costly to maintain law and order.

So why, despite record funding and record numbers of police officers, does this gap exist between public expectations and the kind of policing they are getting?

11

In order to discover this, this report looks at the two areas of policing most in contact with the public. Response police respond to the public in an emergency. Safer Neighbourhood police are part of a new initiative to increase public satisfaction and involvement with the service. It is in the day-to-day experience of these police officers that the unreality of government-speak too often crashes into the reality of unsafe streets, growing youth crime and a police force with its hands tied.

2

Who Responds to Crime?

It starts when the response officer comes on duty. Lights flashing, siren wailing—a response car is what we associate with an emergency.

Response officers are first on the scene of an incident. Outside the Metropolitan Police they are also responsible for the follow-up investigation and preparing all but serious or specialist crimes for court. When not answering emergencies, amongst other duties they take witness statements, collect DNA and look at CCTV footage, give evidence in court, secure a crime scene, ticket motorists and accompany prisoners in custody. Or, as one summed it up: 'We do the job of the social workers, we do the job of the council, the police and the fire brigade.' Response is the sponge that soaks everything up.

Response officers explained the attraction of the job. They enjoy serving the public, the camaraderie of working in a team and the sheer excitement and diversity of dealing with 'the fast-time stuff'. One response officer explained: 'I am a great people watcher. What better place to find out the different facets of peoples' lives but yet still provide a service?' A female response officer described every day as being 'like a box of Quality Street'. They enjoyed being first on the scene to 'people who need help and you are there for them'.

In the 1970s the response car epitomised a new approach to crime using modern technology and better management systems. In practice, as one female response officer explained, 'we rush through the neighbourhood ignoring crime hot spots', and failing to speak to the old lady who needs reassurance. Safer Neighbourhood Policing is meant to address this. Response reacts to crime once it has happened: Safer Neighbourhood Policing seeks to solve issues before they turn into crime. Depending on the force, more and more response officers are moving into Safer Neighbourhood Policing. It is 'flavour of the month with top management', pointed out one response officer, 'which means everything else gets dropped.'

Response officers complained of too few computers, incompatible crime systems, lockers that were falling apart, not enough vehicles or vehicles not repaired swiftly enough ('I have had to put three of my response officers on foot today because there is no vehicle'), stab vests that are too short ('they're in no rush to replace them with proper ones'), and radios that do not work. One officer described finding himself in a house with a mad woman and a failing radio. He said, 'I might as well have had a pigeon.' Another pointed out that Police Community Support Officers (PCSOs) get to wear new fleeces while 'we are still in a woollen jumper and a thin little jacket.'

Response may feel the poor relation but in an emergency it is a response car that the public wants. 'At the end of the day', said one officer, 'if there is no response officers there's no police.' Problem-solving and consultation only go so far. 'The job is sometimes not compatible with being user friendly', explained an officer. 'You've got to be nasty sometimes. You've got to be getting stuck in there.'

Unfortunately it is in response that the problem lies, as the excellent report 'Policing in the Modern Police Organisation—Views from the Front Line' by Michael Chatterton and Emma Bingham, as well as my own research, makes clear.

It starts the moment a response officer comes on duty. Response officers reported regularly turning up at the beginning of a shift to find a third of their fellow officers missing. Twelve forces admitted starting their last shift with only half the number of police who should have been there. 'We've got 13 on every block but we never see 13 people on duty', explained one. 'We only see six or seven turning up.' Another pointed out that ten constables and one sergeant were meant to take care of his area. 'All the time I have been there I've never seen a group—barring Bank Holidays—larger than an acting sergeant and four constables.'

A case study carried out in Basingstoke showed that on one day last year just five officers were covering the town of nearly 150,000 inhabitants.[1] One response officer who actually worked in Basingstoke described that as generous. Many forces do not have a minimum staffing level and few at strategic level 'seems particularly interested'. In fact response officers claimed senior management colluded in covering up the problem of missing officers. A sergeant said he wished the top officers in his force would come down on a Saturday night and see 'what the hell goes on sometimes' because their decisions 'are not based on reality'.

At the same time the government points out that we have never had so many police officers, at around 140,000 full-time equivalent officers in England and Wales as well as some 14,000 PCSOs.

So where are those officers on a Saturday night?

Numbers may be historically high but they are still low compared to other countries. In 2003 there were 264 police officers in England and Wales per 100,000 of the population. This compares to the European average of 357. In New York, where crime has fallen dramatically in the last 20 years, there are approximately 457 police officers per 100,000 of the population and in Chicago 467.[2]

It is not just the numbers of officers that count. It is the numbers of crimes and the ratio between the two. In 1921 there was a ratio of two crimes per officer in England and Wales. One young policeman at his first posting in Chiswick worried that 'he got no cases, and felt that he never would'.[3] By 1981 the ratio of crimes per officer had risen to 23. From 1997 New Labour increased police officer numbers by five per cent— from 127,000 to 134,000. In the same period the number of offences committed rose by 186 per cent. This was partly due to recording crime differently. Even so by 2002/03 the ratio of crimes per officer had risen to an overwhelming 44.[4]

This lack of officers is compounded by what they have to do when on duty. Recent Home Office figures revealed that just 14 per cent of all police officer time is spent on patrol. As in the NHS, a flow of policies, guidelines, objectives and targets from the centre keep officers in the station at their computers. More and more front-line staff are removed from front-line duties to sit in offices counting, checking, auditing and e-mailing.

Quite how much police-time is consumed by these activities emerged from an 'activity-based costing' exercise carried out by the Home Office. In 2005/06 the Metropolitan Police, Britain's biggest force, spent £122.2 million on 'non-incident linked paperwork' and £26.5 million on 'checking paper work' out of a total budget of £3.2 billion. In contrast it spent just £76.6 million on robberies and £48.8 million on house burglaries. It is reassuring to learn that the Met also boasts 'a unit seeking to eliminate unnecessary paperwork'.[5] This paperwork is being done, points out the Police Federation, 'at the expense of response-based policing'. Fewer officers patrolling obviously means short-changing the public. So why is this happening?

One sergeant reeled off the whereabouts of his absent men. Some were on compassionate leave and long-term sickness. Others were on training courses. Yet others had moved to specialist departments such as CID, counter-terrorism, tactical support groups, domestic violence units, family protection posts and Safer Neighbourhood Policing teams. Others had been seconded to proactive teams set up to tackle local problems to enable BCUs (Basic Command Units) meet targets on crime and detections set by the Home Office.

Still others had left to fill posts created by the introduction of new government strategies. These made a long list and included initiatives such as crime management unit personnel, crime and disorder partnership and a prolific and other priority offender units. The officers who leave are not replaced.

One superintendent pointed out that, every time a new unit is set up, 'we have to give people'. When an asset recovery agency was set up in his area 'we thought it was a really good idea. But we lost a sergeant and two PCs to it. Then they set up the joint UK Immigration Service. We have lost half-a-dozen to that. An officer has gone to the Olympics. We have just heard he will be there until 2012.' The superintendent continued: 'Who is left to do the core policing? It's become a very small pool of people and ever-decreasing.'

One response officer recalled what had happened two weeks before in a district with a population of between 70,000 and 80,000. At the start of the 7 a.m. shift not one police officer turned up. 'There wasn't even a sarge ... there wasn't even a constable. They had to send for a PC from another area with a local policing sergeant for supervision. You couldn't get much worse than that!'

No one is arguing against these new initiatives. Each, taken on its own, promises to improve the quality of the policing we receive. Taken as a whole the effect is calamitous. The cost of the reforms in staff time is never calculated. Certainly no attempt is made to increase the numbers of response officers to meet these new demands or work out how their absence affects policing in their area. One response officer tried to explain to an irate old lady why he had taken so long to arrive. 'How many police do you think are on duty in this area tonight?' he asked. 'Seventy or eighty,' she replied, 'Try six!' he said.

Another major problem are the ill thought-out and conflicting targets between the two groups with which response works most closely—call centres and the Crown Prosecution Service (CPS).

Call centres and the CPS have been re-organised to make them more accountable, transparent and efficient for the public. How has this worked out in practice? And how has it affected response?

The first contact a member of the public has with the police is through the call centre. Since the introduction of personal radios, response officers are linked inextricably to their call centres. Call centres exert a huge influence on the work of response officers. They dictate how many jobs an officer gets, how quickly one calls follows another and even the amount of investigative work they have to do afterwards.

Call centres are the gatekeepers to police services. They are the means for police organisations to manage public demand. Not every call is an emergency. Some calls are not police business at all. Others can be dealt with in a few hours or even a few days. To filter calls, call staff need time to question the caller, give advice or refer them elsewhere. They need time to understand a situation from a caller who is often vague, panic stricken or angry.

But time is the last thing that call staff enjoy. Their target dictates they have to deal with 90 per cent of calls in 15 seconds. Investigating a call takes too long. It is far quicker to stick a log on the call, send it to the dispatch centre and get a car out. The log creates a crime. And here is where targets set for call staff are in direct opposition to that of the patrol officer. Patrol officers have to hit so many logs a day. But in order to fulfil their target, call staff are sending on unfiltered calls, creating logs unnecessarily and wasting police time.

In the past, when 'bobbies' were call-handlers, 'they could sort a lot of stuff out there and then on the phone'. Now call-handlers are 'just like robots'. They take the call and put it on the computer, 'and there's got to be a result at the end of the day'.

Officers complain that call staff use stock phrases and fail to question the public robustly. Officers find themselves summoned to a house to fix the heating, pick up a fallen wardrobe or assure an elderly gentleman that he is not being followed by a herd of cats. 'They have their own criteria they have to work to in the control room,' said an officer, 'and that is basically to get rid of jobs as quick as they can. They just give them out willy-nilly.'

Sometimes call staff were in such a hurry that they forgot to get basic information, the right address, the phone number of the caller or even if the situation is dangerous for an officer without a partner. 'You have to call them back', explained an officer crossly, 'when you should be at the scene catching criminals.'

This lack of rigour by call staff left response officers 'slaves to the radio'. It also affected the service they were giving to the public. They received instructions to attend incidents before they had finished dealing with the previous one. Frequently they received jobs in quick succession. 'The controllers just need to get the job off their screen obviously to keep on top of their ticket' explained a response officer. Officers find themselves interviewing a victim about a crime when: 'the communications dispatchers start shouting at you to attend another job. In the middle of dealing with this victim you have to leave suddenly to deal with an emergency. That happens all the time.' Another complained, 'They are pushing you to finish a job because they have others they want to send you to.'

One officer explained how that affects the public. Just before Christmas he was interviewing a woman who had been mugged in the high street. Control dispatched him to other incidents twice. He explained: 'Now that woman was distraught. She had just taken her savings from the bank to get Christmas presents and had the lot stolen.' The officer admitted, 'I felt dreadful. I had to turn around and say "I am going to have to go, I'll be back in a bit". Twice that happened. How is that for quality of service?'

Lack of filtering in the call centre left response officers with a long list of jobs at the start of every shift—'a third of which does not need a police officer' said one impatiently. At 10 a.m. on the morning of one interview, a group of response officers admitted they had 300 jobs waiting—that is 300 members of the public waiting for an officer to attend. Most had 50 to 60 jobs with which to deal. Police felt confident of getting to Grade One Emergency Calls that represent a threat to life and limb. However the management of Grade Two calls—defined as not an immediate threat—'is dubious'.

The longer a job sits in a queue, the less urgent it becomes. The criminal, for example, has run off. This means it can be downgraded. A grade two might need a response within the hour. If there are not enough officers to attend, it is downgraded retrospectively to a grade three. The next day an officer has 'to pick up the pieces from very irate members of the public who expected a response last night and didn't get one'. The public might be irate but the downgrading allows the chief constable to claim, as one response officer said was the case in his force, 'that we're achieving a 95 per cent success rate in our grade one and two responses'.

A sergeant described the effect of this on the police and the public. Three young men had been committing criminal damage in an outlying area. Late one night a man spotted them smashing his fence. He chased the lads away then followed them down the road ringing 999 three times. 'They've completely destroyed my fence, I'm on my own, can you get a police officer to me?' This went on for an hour. No police officer arrived. The caller was apprehensive. The three lads could have turned on him at any time, pulled him out of the car, 'and who knows what'. The call centre achieved its target but at the expense of the police and the victim. Had an officer got there in time, he could have arrested the offenders and reassured the victim. Instead the man had a frightening experience. The police lost his respect and goodwill. It was probably the only occasion he had ever needed the police and they had let him down. Response had also had their workload increased. It took them eight weeks and many man-hours to finally arrest the offenders, clear up the crime and achieve their target.

The effect on the police is clear. They entered the job with an idea of serving the public; instead they spend most of their time 'apologising for things they can't do'. Another commented: 'I am embarrassed by our performance... the public are not getting value for money.' Top officers appear disinterested. They refuse to accept a lack of officers as an excuse for poor performance. They even use strategies to make the number of officers available appear larger than it is. Officers involved in specialist operations, for example, are actually counted as response even if they never turn up for duty. The figures might look good but in the end it does not change reality. As one officer remarked, 'There ain't no magic button you press and scores of officers come shooting out.'

This lack of interest from top officers and politicians puzzled the ordinary response officer. 'They must know there are not enough police,' stated one, 'They must know we are overworked.' It does not matter what picture they portray to the public, 'they must know, surely?' His colleague put him right. They may know but it does not matter if 'their constituents and the British public don't know'. And there is the nub.

23

Policing, like health, has become a political football. What is right for politicians today is not necessarily right for those institutions tomorrow—or for the public they serve.

3

Problems with the Crown Prosecution Service

Many police were bitter that they are blamed for short-comings of the criminal justice system. A victim of crime does not judge a crime in isolation: they judge the judicial process. Did the police arrive swiftly? Did they track down the criminal and was that criminal brought to justice? Did the culprit get a fair sentence and how much of that sentence did they serve? Unfortunately none of the many targets set by the government reflect the experience of the victim.

A belief in the fairness of the criminal justice system is integral to our society. Politicians depend on that belief for a mandate to rule. The loss of trust in a country's justice system is serious for any democracy. Our judicial system is not like transport or health, where a decline in performance is obvious in cancelled trains or dirty hospitals. Its disintegration, as Norman Dennis and George Erdos point out in their excellent book *Cultures and Crimes* is diffuse and invisible.[1]

The extent of the problems facing our criminal justice system is clear from the government's own figures. The Criminal Statistics report reveals how the criminal justice system dealt with each of the 5,428,000 crimes recorded by the police last year. Of that total the police solved 1,475,000. Forty-seven per cent, or 693,250 offenders, were charged or summonsed to appear in court. The Crown Prosecution Service either dropped or discontinued 287,250 cases. So out of 693,250 only 406,000 arrived in court. Some 303,000 finally reached the point where they were sentenced by a judge or magistrate, of whom 74,000 were jailed.

To ease prison overcrowding, more and more criminals are receiving fines, community punishments or fixed penalty notices. Of the 1,475,000 crimes which police managed to solve in 2006, 350,000 received a caution—an increase of 17 per cent. One in four burglars—7,700 offenders—and 58 per cent of violent attackers (57,000 offenders) also got nothing more than a caution. So did 28 per cent of sex offenders—including 24 rapists.[2]

It is not surprising the public displays little confidence in the criminal justice system. In November 2007 the British Crime Survey discovered only half of those questioned believed the CPS was effective in bringing criminals to justice. Sixty per cent doubted it dealt with cases promptly and efficiently. Sixty-seven per cent did not believe it met the needs of victims while 64 per cent had little faith that it reduced crime. Seventy-five per cent thought it ineffective in dealing with young people accused of crime; 79 per cent believed sentencing was too lenient and 40 per cent of those believed it 'much too lenient'. It is a damning indictment of our criminal justice system. Any company enjoying such little public confidence would have gone out of business long ago.[3] Unfortunately it is the criminal justice system as a whole by which the police are too often judged.

The only contact the majority of us have with the law is as motorists. Unlike the rest of our criminal justice system, here punishment is certain, swift and effective. In my street, for example, you cannot leave your car three minutes over-time before receiving a ticket. But you can—as the yellow board put up by police in my road testified last year—get away with murder.

Two-thirds of the public in a 2007 survey believed that the police preferred to focus on easy targets such as speeding motorists rather than anti-social behaviour and local crime.[4] No one is arguing against punishing motorists who break the speed limit, but the police appear to have lost their discretion. One policeman explained why. He used to book motorists doing 11 miles per hour over the speed limit. 'Every traffic cop has their own line. That was mine.' But motorists in his area became more careful. Far from rejoicing at this good news, his superior officers complained revenues were tumbling. So, 'in order to keep revenues up', he had to book motorists doing a few miles over the limit. He pointed out that, if people obeyed the law, 'I don't have a job'.

Even within motor offences, punishment is in inverse proportion to the severity of the crime. On 10 December 2007 a court heard how a 27-year-old man knocked over a three year old girl who was crossing the road with her mother. The man was driving a stolen car at 48 mph in a 30 mph zone. He had no licence. For driving illegally in a stolen car, failing to stop at the scene of an accident, killing a child and leaving the mother screaming in horror at the road side, he received a sentence of 12 weeks in prison—of which he served just six weeks.

After he was freed, he went on to breach his five-year driving ban four times, including twice in one day. A spokesman for the road safety charity Brake said: 'Justice and punishment are meant to act as a deterrent—his 12-week sentence obviously didn't act as one. It was an insult to the little girl's death and has obviously had no affect on him.'[5]

In order to bring an offender to justice the police work with the Crown Prosecution Service. Outside London, response officers also investigate their cases, interviewing witnesses, gathering forensic evidence and preparing the case for the Crown Prosecution Service to bring to trial. One female response officer described the experience: 'It's like preparing a good recipe, hunting out special ingredients and then having nothing to cook it in.' Another summed up the general view of nearly every policeman interviewed: 'It's an absolutely barking system.'

As with call centres, the police find their targets in conflict with those of the CPS, to the detriment of the public. CPS lawyers are judged, amongst other things, by the proportion and volume of successful convictions. This supposedly sensible target has two unintended consequences.

The Crown Prosecution Service should be fair, independent and objective. It should not be influenced by undue pressure from any source. In practice this objectivity is compromised by their performance assessment regime.

In order to meet their target, CPS lawyers only bring to court those cases they are fairly sure of winning. In order to do so they will test 'every drunk to the level of a terrorist', complained one sergeant, and collect 'every single, tiny scrap of evidence'. Before, if the police caught a well known shop-lifter, provided they got a statement from the store detective, 'we would run with it. Nine times out of ten he would hold his hands up in court. Job dealt with.'

Now, for a CPS conscious of its targets, one statement from a witness is not enough. They want statements from three or four people working in the shop, CCTV evidence and even forensics. At the trial, the defendant admits his guilt. The CPS claims it is because they have arrived in court prepared. The police remain unconvinced. 'Most career criminals would anyway', one officer explained.

Investigating each case at such length helps CPS solicitors fulfil their targets but it has, like the targets for call centres, 'massive resource implications' for the police. CPS solicitors are not accountable for the amount of police time they use. They can demand, as one officer recalls, '15 statements three times each' from 15 different witness. Nobody is arguing against the desire of the CPS to win as many cases as possible. The problem is nobody has weighed up whether this is the best use of the already over-stretched response officer.

It is not just getting the evidence. A visit to a CPS solicitor also takes time. If there is no CPS based in their station, the response officer has to travel to the appointment. A sergeant described what happens in his area. In order to make an appointment, an officer has to put his name up on the board in the CPS office. The CPS will not accept bookings by telephone. The officer has to drive, in his area between seven to 20 miles, just to reserve a time. If a slot exists and depending on the time, the officer has to wait or come back later. Two hours is not an unusual wait. 'So,' the sergeant continued, 'you can write him off for five hours just to get CPS advice.' That is five hours when he could have been out on patrol.

Often the officer will need to see the CPS more than once for the same case. 'You can guarantee that you're never going to see the same CPS lawyer twice', said one officer. This means waiting while they read through the file. At the end of which: 'You'll get told two different stories'. Even then the hapless officer is dispatched to collect more evidence, 'just for the CPS to prove why they will not take my case to court'.

As one Sector Support Inspector said: 'We've got performance indicators to try and meet and so have the CPS. But they seem to be… going apart rather than going together.'

The CPS target also brings them into conflict with the interests of the victim. Many police officers felt bitter about the number of cases the CPS dropped. Police complained a case had to be 'water-tight' for CPS to proceed, otherwise they put their target in jeopardy. 'Are they entitled to demand that?' questioned one policeman, 'They are supposed to be taking a case and arguing it in court, aren't they? Let the bench decide whether this person is guilty.'

The career criminal is perfectly well aware of the reluctance of the CPS to charge. 'They actually admit that to us', said one officer bitterly. 'They know that they can go out and commit the same offences again and again and again.' One young man he had recently arrested said: '"Well everything else I've been arrested for has been an NFA (No Further Action). So this will be as well." He's laughing at us.'

CPS solicitors appear to be putting their own performance targets before the best interests of the victim. It is officers and not the CPS who must break the news that a case is being dropped. It is they who experience the frustration, anger and despair of the victims. 'We're the ones', said one response officer angrily, 'who have to go and tell them that mum's dead, dad's dead and by the way the bloke who beat you up has been NFA'd (No Further Action) because he always gets away with it.'

One detective explained the implications for the public over the long term. Each time the police catch a criminal, he learns how he was caught, and he 'won't make that mistake again.' The police, for example, catch a burglar by the footprint he left in the garden. So next time he throws away his trainers. The detective recalled finally arresting a serial sex offender. He had shaved every part of his body, wore rubber gloves, a large condom and never allowed himself even a lick of the victim. 'He didn't just decide to be a bit of a weirdo,' explained the detective. He had learnt from all the previous occasions he had been caught and let off. The detective went on: 'Each time you catch them, each time they are let off, it becomes harder and harder to catch them again.'

A detective summed up the situation, 'We are trying to catch the bad guys against odds stacked against us from inside the organisation.'

The CPS target also has serious implications for the most vulnerable in our society who can make poor witnesses. Too often those most in need of a champion are least likely to get it in the CPS. A woman working as a prostitute was raped by a client. It was premeditated. He had a rope ready to tie her up and the implements to torture her with. Her ordeal lasted four-and-a-half hours. Her injuries were so serious she had to have a total hysterectomy. Nine months later the same man raped another escort girl. The CPS refused to take the case to court because of 'insufficient evidence'. The woman brought a private prosecution, the first for rape in England. Her attacker was found guilty on the same evidence that the CPS had dismissed as insufficient and sentenced to 14 years. It was reduced on appeal to 11. He eventually served seven years.[6]

That was over ten years ago but has much changed? A detective described the effect of the CPS target on one 12-year-old girl who had been raped. She lied to the police about how she had met her attacker. She claimed he was a stranger, when in fact she had met him on a blind date arranged by her brother. It was her first date and she was a virgin. She was illiterate and so were most of her family. The police warned the CPS she might make an unreliable witness. The CPS, according to the police, failed to act on this information until the first day of the trial. Suddenly they dropped the case. The family were devastated. The detective continued: 'The CPS wanted us to tell the family. We refused. We insisted a solicitor tell the mother and daughter they were pulling the plug.' Her attacker then tried to sue the police but was caught raping his nine-month-old niece. The detective added: 'He's now doing life. And about time.' As another officer admitted, the CPS are 'demoralising our morale ... they will just bin jobs.'

The decision on how to charge a suspect is also based on the ease of getting a conviction. In order to hit their targets for successful prosecutions, CPS lawyers often downgrade crimes.

One sector support inspector gave an example. A man entered a house with an iron bar, walked up stairs, pulled the bedclothes off a woman and brandished the bar at her. The police put the crime down as an aggravated burglary. The CPS changed it to the much less serious charge of possessing an offensive weapon with affray. The inspector was incandescent. A career criminal such as this burglar, he insisted, should be dealt with correctly. He should not be prosecuted for just any offence that allows the CPS, 'to get a conviction off the court'. Another officer commented: 'We had one 'threat to kill' that ended up as 'breach of the peace'.

An officer found himself a victim of the CPS. He arrested a man who then tried to knock him out and escape. The man denied throwing the punch and the CPS dropped the charge, 'and I am thinking, hold on, that's not very good service to me'. The officer went on: 'I've got a family. I am not there as a punching bag and the fact that the CPS don't give a crap about me I think is plain appalling.' Welcome to the club.

The failure of the CPS is part of a larger failure of the criminal justice system to deal with repeat offenders. The latest figures (2003) show 61 per cent of offenders were reconvicted within two years. This rose to 73 per cent of young offenders between the ages of 18-21 and a shocking 82 per cent of male adolescents (15 to 18). Peter Fahy, Chief Constable of Cheshire, blamed the criminal justice system for failing to protect victims and failing to rehabilitate persistent offenders. He said: 'it's the same small proportion of people causing problems... It's that group of people the criminal justice system needs to be able to address.'[7]

Chief Superintendent Dominic Clout, Borough Commander for Kensington & Chelsea, summed up the views of nearly every policeman interviewed. The police are doing their job, 'charging and gaining convictions', only to see the same people before the judge over and over again. 'All I have to do is pick up the pieces when it doesn't work. That's what police do—clean up the mess.' He continued: 'But it's me who has to go in front of the public meeting and answer questions about crime rates. You don't get probation officers going before those meetings; you don't get district judges having to publicly justify their actions.'[8]

4

When Targets Distort Policing: Sanctioned Detections

The police too have their targets. The most controversial is sanctioned detections and the pressure on the police to achieve a certain number each month. This was bitterly resented by the police interviewed. It skews police activity. It means they concentrate on minor crimes rather than the more complex; it takes away their discretion; most of all it alienates the public. One patrol officer complained that when he issues a fine, the public now demand: 'How many points does that get you?' An inspector pointed out that ill-considered targets injudiciously applied 'ultimately impact upon the solid and well earned respect of the communities we serve'.

A sanctioned detection or judicial disposal are offences detected or cleared by charging someone, issuing a PND (penalty notice) or giving them a caution if they will admit the offence, have no previous record and have not recently received a PND. In other words, targets measure crime committed rather than crime prevented. 'Policing is fundamentally about problem solving', wrote one constable to a Police Forum. If disputes can be resolved before an arrest is necessary, 'then we make more friends than enemies within our communities'. It is this element of policing that performance indicators not only disregard but actually undermine.

The pressure to get sanctioned detections is in direct response to government policy. In April 2005 Hazel Blears told MPs that the government had 'made clear' its desire to achieve a sanctioned detection rate of 25 per cent by 2007/08. 'A major drive' was underway to do so and 'to address unacceptable variations in detections performance between forces'.

Basic Command Unit (BCU) commanders are judged by their rate of sanctioned detections. These commanders are held accountable by the chief officers in the force who are themselves accountable to the Home Office—sometimes on a daily basis—for a slide in figures. Their bonuses of £10,000 to £15,000 depend on achieving certain targets which include sanctioned detection numbers. An officer described the style of management this produces. The commander goes to headquarters and gets, 'a bollocking in front of the others' for not hitting his targets. When he comes back 'that bollocking passes down the line'. In those circumstances justifying a failure to meet the target with: '"Well sorry but I was helping the public instead" just doesn't wash'.

In fact BCU Commanders share their officers' concerns, as a survey for the excellent report *Fitting the Bill*, published by Policy Exchange, makes clear.[1] A staggering 71 per cent of BCU Commanders believed that Home Office reporting requirements had a negative effect on the quality of policing. 'My value', admitted one, 'is reflected in a small number of figures for my division which have become the defining factors between success and failure. Any views which offer an alternative approach are not listened too.'[2]

BCU Commanders find themselves in the same position as the managers of an NHS hospital. Government driven agendas require immediate attention and action. Each day brings a new initiative from the Home Office or Department of Health. Targets change at a whim. This means the priorities of both police and health managers are in constant flux. Their attention is wholly focused on the demands of the centre rather than the needs of the public.

A BCU Commander complained that none of his chief officer team had ever worked in a BCU commander post. They did not understand the balancing act between targets such as sanctioned detections and Safer Neighbourhood Policing. They failed to see the conflict between the short-term performance outcomes wanted by the Home Office and the long-term problem solving desired by the public. He added: 'The system is so unsophisticated it is worthless.'[3]

In order to meet targets, police are now classifying incidents as crimes that would previously have been dealt with informally, classified differently or ignored. To understand the effect of targets on police activity, look no further than Section 5 of the Public Order Act 1986.

Section 5 allows the police to arrest anyone for 'threatening, abusive or insulting words or behaviour within the sight of a person likely to be caused harassment, alarm or distress'. A senior policeman explained that before the arrival of sanctioned detections, the police only evoked section 5 for a public order offence, 'a full-blown punch-up' was how he put it. Targets have changed that. The police can now claim a sanctioned detection for an arrest under Section 5. Suddenly minor crime and even innocuous activities appear in a different light. Many police complained senior officers were pressurising them to make arrests they considered unethical.

An officer was called to a park. A woman had seen some children playing around with a tree. He found the tree undamaged. He radioed in: 'There is no crime. Just kids messing about.' This was unwelcome news to the crime desk. They announced there was a crime and it was harassment under Section 5. They wanted the officer to claim a sanctioned detection. 'For harassing a tree?' he asked in consternation. No, for harassing the woman, reproved the crime desk, unwilling to let the chance of a sanctioned detection disappear. She was obviously distressed by the children. It took the officer two or three hours and a number of 'snotty' e-mails to get the crime desk to change their minds.

Two officers were watching CCTV tapes when one noted a young woman caught by the camera peeing modestly behind a bush on some waste ground at 3 a.m. His colleague was all for labelling it a Section 5, tracking down the woman and charging her. The other officer pointed out she was on her own. There was no one around to be distressed. 'But that's how a lot of police think now', he said. Another explained that if he caught someone urinating in public on a Saturday night, he was supposed to issue a fixed penalty notice under section 5. This earned him a sanctioned detection. 'I adamantly refuse,' he declared. 'Urinating in a public place is not section 5. It's a specific offence. I'll report them by way of a summons.' But that does not earn his force a sanctioned detection. He added: 'I've been hauled over the coals for it.' It is not just unethical, it is an absurd waste of police time.

Another officer does the early shift at weekends. He looks at the statements from drunks sobering up in the cells arrested for Section 5 'and sometimes you're wincing. You are thinking, how is this Section 5?' He knows if any of them chose to plead not guilty and go to court 'the (arresting) officer would struggle'.

A patrol officer described what happened to the drunks in his town when senior officers realised they could be arrested under Section 5 instead.

Suddenly in a town with a large student population there were no drunks. The drunk and disorderly were still being arrested but not for inebriation. The exception proved to be the railway station because the transport police, 'were not playing the game'. There the number of drunks shot up. 'Odd that', mused the officer.

He described a typical incident. A drunken student was dancing amongst the municipal flowerbeds. 'Arrest him under Section 5!' came the order over the radio. 'He's not doing any damage', answered the patrol officer. The student had taken aim at a sunflower and gone for the goal only to fall over before hitting it. 'He's causing alarm and distress to the public!' admonished the crime desk. 'Well everyone here is laughing themselves silly', retorted the patrol officer. He went on: 'It was all just youthful exuberance'.

Over a twelve-month period the force re-classified just under 2,000 drunk and disorderly arrests as Section 5. Any police officer who refused to collude was disciplined. At the end of the year the force had dramatically improved its rankings. Sanctioned detections had shot up. This delighted the chief constable and ensured his bonus. It also pleased the Home Office who could announce the police were catching more and more criminals.

Then a new crime manager took over. He was scandalised. It was, he emphasised, not only unethical but illegal. The patrol officer pointed out the consequences for a student arrested under Section 5 rather than for being drunk and disorderly. A prospective employer looks at criminal records. He might accept a night in the cells for being intoxicated. 'Well, we've all done that.' He would view an arrest under Section 5 in a different light. 'Mouthing off at the police, alarming the public—what does that say about your attitude towards authority?' The arrest could seriously affect a young person's career. The officer said his force had refused to admit they had done anything wrong, let alone apologise.

This concentration on minor crime comes at the expense of the more serious incident. Crimes that would have been previously written off are now subject to extended investtigation and paperwork. 'We have become crime reporters rather than crime investigators,' said one officer sadly. All of which removes the response officer from the street.

One inspector pointed out the anomaly between those actions that earn a sanctioned detection and those that do not. Arresting a child for chalking on the pavement, as happened in his force recently, gets a sanctioned detection. The painstaking, time-consuming work of tracking down a missing child does not. A child stealing a Mars bar earns the officer the same as a murder. Murders obviously require a lot more police time than a Mars bar—'30 policemen, hundreds of hours' said one detective of the last murder he had investigated. Officers are now reluctant to get involved in police work that does not earn a target. 'We put less effort into areas we are not judged on.'

This is often the very police work that the public appreciates—reassurance and solving problems. Advising an old lady on better security; spending 'seven hours with a victim of crime' as one officer had done that week; giving a youth a stern talking-to; comforting the family where someone has died suddenly; or reassuring a woman that wolves were not about to break through her walls. None of these fulfils a single target, yet for the public they are the essence of good policing.

Home Office targets even fail to measure specialists within a force. A firearms officer was incensed to discover how his men were judged. It was not on their shooting skills, managing a firearms incident or anything else to do with their specialist training. Instead it was how many sanctioned detections they had made. Firearms officers are part of a response team when not on an incident. The officer who gets the most sanctioned detections is not necessarily the best firearms officer, it is simply the one with the most opportunity to give a caution or make an arrest. Those officers involved in a firearms incident or on a course to improve their skills lose out.

The firearms officer described a recent job. Bank robbers had held up a number of armoured vans collecting cash from a local shopping mall. He and his men patrolled the mall, flak jackets on, guns in hand. 'So how are we meant to get our quota of sanctioned detections?' he asked. 'Was I supposed to stop a speeding motorist and ask him to hold my gun while I took down his name and address?'

He went on: 'I could be a sniper sitting on a roof for two days. That work is not counted towards my targets. All they say is, why are your ticket rates down?' He pointed out that no member of the public had ever been shot by the police in his area. 'Well isn't that a good thing? It's taken for granted and certainly not measured.' He went on, 'You are a writer. How would you like to be judged on something else altogether—like how many widgets you made last week?'

The firearms officer decided to produce his own targets. As he explained: 'The officers' responsibility is to make optimum use of their time. The manager's responsibility is to direct it.' He worked out a valuation system that took into account time spent, tasks performed and quality of service. He ranked his men according to his method then compared his ranking to that of the division. The same officers tended to appear in the middle of both sets of tables. But a number of men at the bottom of the division's tables appeared at the top of his. He considered them some of his best officers. Home Office ratings had failed to take into account their skill or the care with which they served the public. Had he told them how they were rated officially? He shook his head, 'I don't expose my officers to that,' he explained, 'they would feel very undervalued and disillusioned.'

Targets should help police forces differentiate between good and bad officers. This, as the firearms officer had discovered, they fail to do. It is not for lack of technical wizardry or money. One force displayed impressive graphs illustrating the divisional performance review of every officer. The lines representing the activity, including sanctioned detections, of some officers stretched across the page. Others barely registered. Were these very good or very bad officers?

One officer had attended only seven incidents in five months. He had made no stop-and-searches, given out no penalty notices (PNDs), investigated no crimes, made no intelligent reports and failed to interview a single person. Another had done even less. He had managed just one intelligence report over the same period. Yet both men received glowing reports from their sergeants. The second man even got a recommendation for a job in CID. Was his sergeant using promotion to get rid of him? Had his reassurance policing gone unrecorded? Was he moonlighting on a second job? Or was his sergeant simply covering up for a weak officer who nonetheless always backed him up in a fight on a Saturday night? The graph gave no indication.

A deputy chief constable admitted the number of police who had actually lost their jobs over targets was 'miserable'. He went on: 'The system is not as tough as the police make it out to be. It certainly has not cut swathes through the ranks of the police.'

Targets also contribute to our surreal system of youth justice. On the one hand our courts and police are unable or unwilling to deal with gangs. On the other the police criminalise adolescents of previously good character in order to raise sanctioned detections. 'We fiddle the figures something chronic', said one constable cheerfully.

Gangs of youths are one of the biggest fears of the public. They are right to be fearful. Violent crime carried out by children and teenagers has increased by one-third over three years. The number of under-18-year-olds convicted or cautioned over violent offences rose from 17,590 to 24,102—an increase of 37 per cent over the same period. Robberies went by up 43 per cent. By contrast adult convictions and cautions increased by less than one per cent.

The police and the criminal justice system appear powerless to deal with gangs of violent youths, as the Newlove family discovered to their cost. At the trial of the five teenagers accused of her husband's murder,

45

Helen Newlove described how police failed to do anything about local gangs despite numerous complaints from residents. Youths would gather at the subway only yards from their house, drinking, being noisy and vandalising cars. 'They began to urinate against the fence and hide from the police in the passageway', she told the court. To them it was a game. They had no fear of the police—rightly as it turned out. At resident meetings police claimed they lacked resources. Mrs Newlove continued: 'Meetings would become heated and nothing would be done.'[4]

Even when the police do arrest a violent young offender, more than half are let off with a caution. Adam Swellings, convicted of beating to death Garry Newlove, was a repeat violent offender. A police officer whose daughter was assaulted by Swellings claims that the justice system has 'lost sight' of its mission.[5]

A study by the Centre for Crime and Justice Studies shows that knifepoint robberies have doubled in the last two years from 25,500 in 2005 to 64,000 in the year to April 2007. The CCJS figures mean that, on average, in the past year there were 175 knife robberies a day on the streets of England and Wales.[6] The majority of victims are other youths. When I did a survey of crime in my neighbourhood, 17 out of the 20 households interviewed had suffered mugging and assaults over the previous three years—seven on women and ten on children under 16.

An American neighbour's experience was typical. Her fifteen-year-old son was attacked by three boys in hoods, threatened with a knife and punched in the face. 'It was very humiliating, very difficult. He came home and fell apart.' She found the police 'sympathetic' but it was only 'lip service. They go away and nothing happens.' She talked to other mothers at school whose sons had similar experiences. 'How come people are so complacent about the stuff happening to our kids on the street? Getting beaten up is not a rite of passage that I find acceptable. A first kiss should be a rite of passage.' She found it hard to live in a city 'with this insecurity. Inside of me I rage.'

In this situation, what are the police doing? Rather than concentrating on persistent and violent youth offenders, they are busy creating crime to government orders. Minor crime, a retired inspector explained, is going on all the time. Police merely 'pluck something out of the air' in order to detect it and so fulfil targets.

To get their quota at the end of the month, many forces admitted they go for the easy option. In one force it was the local university. Police in search of a cannabis detection stop a student and check his pockets. The guilty student admits possession, receives a caution and that five minutes of work earns the equivalent of a murder or burglary detection. Certainly it is a lot easier than dealing with a gang of violent youths. 'We deal with the easy ones', explained an officer. 'We do what we can in order not to solve the crime or detect it but get rid of it.' Another admitted the police should be going into the college and educating the students on the effects of smoking cannabis. But: 'we know that there's some nice detections to be had there every month. It's like why get rid of our detections by educating people?'

The effect of sanctioned detections is indeed to catch young males—but not the ones that count. One sergeant said: 'I could guarantee that if I watched anyone's son hard enough, I could pick him up for something—scrawling his name in felt tip on a bus stop, playing rugby in the street. They all do something. It's hormones.' Another admitted he warned his 16-year-old son to take extra care at the end of the month—when police are looking to fill their quota.

A patrol officer said: 'The worst of it is we are not locking up the real offenders.' Another explained that the repeat youth offender knows the system: 'He'll get off.' But not the respectable and otherwise well behaved. He continued sadly: 'We are bringing more and more people to justice but they are the wrong people.'

In the process the police are criminalising a generation. They can issue a young man of previously good character with a caution—for which the police receive a sanctioned detection. Police admit they push youngsters to admit to the offence in exchange 'for only getting a caution'. This is misleading or, as one officer put it, 'unethical behaviour'.

A caution involves an arrest. Everyone arrested gives a sample of DNA which automatically guarantees a criminal record number on the Police National Computer. A criminal record number affects a young person taking up certain occupations (joining the police for one) and getting a USA visa. One senior police officer confirmed: 'We are in discussions with the Americans to make them aware of our system.' The Americans find it difficult to understand that a number of our criminals are not criminal at all—simply a result of Home Office targets.

A typical casualty of this policy is Gregorio, 19 years old, half-Italian, half-American and a student at SOAS university. On his way home with a friend before Christmas, he had no plans to take part in any criminal activity. It was midnight and the lift doors at Russell Square tube station were closing. Gregorio rushed forward and put his foot between the doors to hold them open. He and his friend jumped in, apologising to the two men already in the lift. 'No worries', they replied.

Suddenly a bell went off. An official turned up and ordered Gregorio to take the stairs. 'Come on, nothing happened', protested the young man. The official threatened to call the police. He also forbade Gregorio's friend from going with him. The men already in the lift protested, astonished at the reaction of the official. Gregorio shrugged. His friend, ignoring the man's order, joined Gregorio on the long walk down to the platform where the last train waited. They got in and sat down. A minute went by and then another.

Suddenly the reason why the train did not leave became clear. Three transport police arrived on the platform, arrested Gregorio and took him back upstairs. There they handed him over to three officers from the Met. The officers handcuffed Gregorio's hands behind his back and put him in a van. They told his friend he was not allowed to stay with Gregorio. At the police station the custody suite was full, so the young man, accompanied by the three policemen, waited in the van for over an hour.

Finally Gregorio was led through the criminal entrance to the custody desk. Here his rights were read to him, his shoe-laces and other personal things removed and he was put in a cell with a toilet and a camera watching him. It was now 2 a.m. He had his fingerprints and DNA taken and was offered a solicitor who never actually turned up. 'I talked to him on the phone but his accent was so strong I could barely understand him.'

Before a taped interview he learnt he was not guilty of a criminal offence but of breaking a community by-law—stopping a lift from moving. Gregorio pointed out that the lift had not yet begun to move. The doors were still closing. That was the whole point. The police shrugged. Of course he could go to court, they said. But if he just admitted his guilt, he would receive a caution and go home. By now it was 5 a.m. Gregorio chose the caution. Half an hour later he was finally on his way home.

This story is hardly, as one policeman put it, one of 'quality of service to the public.' It does reveal the bizarre stratagems created by the target culture. In a city were knife crime is exploding and the public are crying out for more police on the streets, three officers are tied up for half the night arresting a young man for holding a lift door open with his foot. How much would I, as a member of the public, like just one of those police with me at 1 a.m. when I cross the estate near my house. But then I have no say in how I am policed. Nobody asks me if this is the best use of scarce resources. The arrest of Gregorio had nothing to do with reassuring the public, keeping the peace or pursuing criminals. It had everything to do with securing a sanctioned detection. As Gregorio himself remarked, there was 'a minimal sense of reality' about the experience.

Sanctioned detections undermine the relationship between the police and the public at every turn. One casualty less appreciated by the public but prized by the police is discretion. 'The most important tool on an officer's belt' explained one officer, and the most useful 'in maintaining trust and support within our communities.'

A police officer of many years' experience explained what he did when he caught a young boy shoplifting for the first time or damaging a garden fence. He would take him back to his parents. 'I know these estates', he said. 'I was brought up on one.' If the mother laid into her son 'I took it no further. Young lads have to kick off. You don't criminalise them for it.' Those days are gone. It is much more difficult for officers to exercise discretion. Now everything has to have a crime number and be part of the performance culture. Imagine, said one officer, setting a target for fire fighters. They have to use a high pressure hose on 45 per cent of their jobs. Then watch them get a cat out of a tree. That is the position in which targets have placed the police.

Officers viewed discretion as an important tool in community policing. One conjured an almost mythical past before the advent of targets and health and safety legislation. He had worked in the area where he lived. His use of discretion meant on those nights when he found himself short of back up, 'the locals would help out if you had a fight on the go' because previously 'you had told them when they were playing up to "GO HOME"'.

A firearms officer found himself outside a school monitoring the traffic. He flagged down a middle-aged man for not wearing a seat belt. He managed to resist the temptation 'to alienate the police service further by scoring five easy points' and, after some advice, let the man go. A few months later he found himself in an unoccupied house where a gun had been found 'in highly suspicious circumstances'. As he was wondering what to do next, a man approached him—the same one from the seat belt incident. He was able to provide information that saved 'several hours' of police investigation. The officer continued: 'And he was happy to help me because he had been dealt with fairly.' The officer went on: 'Would he have felt the same if I had not used my discretion? We should be left to use common sense on the streets.'

This was a view shared by many. An exasperated officer asserted it was time to stop following 'half-baked ideas and requirements from the Home Office'. Instead, 'let's show those criminals how good we are'.

Then the general public 'might start having a bit more faith in the system... and not ridicule us for well documented arrests that, frankly, I would be ashamed of.'

Exactly why officers have had to jettison discretion along with common sense and public respect is summed up by an e-mail sent to each officer in a division. It pointed out that the group had under-performed again that month regarding sanctioned detections. It continued: 'The inspector has asked that you each provide a full report outlining the reason why the three sanctioned detections required by each officer have not been achieved.' This should include 'how you are going to achieve the detections this month'. It emphasised the inspector wanted these ideas 'to be written in depth as he is not happy how the block is performing compared to everyone else.' The report had to be completed and submitted by the end of each officer's tour of duty.

5

Does Safer Neighbourhood Policing Help?

It is against this background of scarce resources and ill thought-out targets that the government has launched Safer Neighbourhood Policing. It is an attempt to bridge the gap between the policing that we want and the policing we get. The government aims to increase public satisfaction and involvement with the police. In 2005 the government made the commitment that every area in England and Wales 'will benefit from dedicated, visible, accessible and responsive Safer Neighbourhood Policing teams'. By 2007 we should all have seen increased patrolling, better local information and a greater focus on confidence and reassurance.

The Home Office wants every electoral ward in the country to be covered by a dedicated Safer Neighbourhood Policing team by 2008. Some forces have embraced the concept more quickly than others. London, for example, enjoys Safer Neighbourhood Teams in all of its local authority wards. These teams consist of six officers—one sergeant, two constables and three Police Community Support Officers (PCSOs). Their brief is to make people feel safe and secure by reducing crime and anti-social behaviour in the area.

They do this by simply walking around their neighbourhoods. When I accompanied two PCSOs on the estate near my house, they pointed to a triangle of open space. The summer before people complained of gangs of youths gathering there. The PCSOs noticed a pole on which the young people liked to sit. 'So we asked the council to take it down.' The result was immediate. The young people vanished. 'Except', added one PCSO, 'now they complain to me they have nowhere to sit!'

Safer Neighbourhood Policing is an admirable initiative. It aims to get police out of their cars and stations and back on the streets and into their communities. It emphasises prevention. 'No more riding around in cars waiting for something to happen, or sending a car after something has happened', said George Kelling, the academic behind the 'Broken Windows' theory and the transformation of New York policing.[1]

Every police force needs Emergency Response units. But they should not be the only strategy to deal with crime. A leading exponent of Safer Neighbourhood Policing in this country and a policeman himself explained: 'My firm view is that it is the most important part of policing. You can't do anything else without public confidence and you can only win that through Safer Neighbourhood Policing.' Safer Neighbourhood Policing is the government's answer to public disenchantment with the way they are policed locally. Is it going to work?

That the public are not happy is clear. An ICM survey commissioned by the Taxpayer's Alliance in April of 2007 showed that, despite the huge amounts of investment in policing and anti-crime measures, just 23 per cent of the public feel that the service has improved in their area. Trust in the police is now lower than in doctors, teachers, judges or the NHS. More than half did not think that increases in council tax to pay for improvements to local policing had been good value for money. They believed fewer police walked the beat despite the record number of officers in the force. Worryingly, the majority of people have little connection with their local force. Few know the name of a police officer or are able to identify the head of the police authority.[2]

The lack of communication between the public and their local force is widespread and startling. Safer Neighbourhood Policing depends on a more transparent relationship between the police and their local communities. Community engagement is crucial. Talking to local residents is still, however, an alien concept for many police forces. Take two very different areas: a wealthy local authority in London and a run-down town elsewhere in the county.

The London authority is strong on Safer Neighbourhood Policing, low in crime and interested in the views of its residents. It takes a detailed Residents Panel Survey every year. Nonetheless 72 per cent of those questioned last year felt 'not very well informed' or 'not very well informed at all' about the Council's plans to tackle anti-social behaviour in their local area. Only 39 per cent of respondents reported having heard of the Safer Neighbourhood Policing programme.

Even less knew of the various consultation groups between the police and local residents. The Police and

Community Consultative Group, for example, 'aims to bring policing closer to the community' at ward level. Police officers and police community support officers meet with a panel of local residents and businesses to help set priorities for the team. Unfortunately only 22 per cent of residents had heard of it. Only 18 per cent had heard of the Safer Neighbourhood Panel and eight per cent of the Police Sector Working Groups. Apart from the Panel, these percentages had all decreased or had stayed the same since the previous year.

The majority of the London authority residents did not know how to influence policing in their community. They did not even know they could. But they were clear on what they wanted. As one said: 'We need to see more police in uniform patrolling the streets during the day and at night. I have never seen a police officer in my area.'

In a very different part of the country, senior officers did a performance review of a run-down town in their area. This was part of a presentation to local managers on the need for Safer Neighbourhood Policing. It opened with a series of photographs showing a broken playground, a smashed phone box and a public notice board empty of any notices. The survey asked residents how many police they saw patrolling on foot as opposed to in cars. Over half had only seen police in cars. A third rated the presence of police patrols as 'very poor'. As one resident remarked: 'police on foot here—its like dodo shit'.

Senior officers asked the same questions as the local authority in London. The answers proved equally depressing. Nobody in the run-down town knew the name of the district inspector or the superintendent. Over 90 per cent did not know their local police officer. Less than 15 per cent could name their local PCSOs. Further inquiry revealed that of those who could, all knew just one, obviously hard working, PCSO described as: 'The girl with the pony tail who is always up and down here'.

Residents were asked, apart from dialling 999, if they knew how to contact their local police station. Eighty-four per cent had no idea. Fourteen per cent offered a number that turned out to be defunct. Not one resident had any knowledge of their Community Neighbourhood Panels. As one remarked: 'I think something like that happens but I don't know when.'

For those of us who do know how to contact our local police, it is still difficult to extract even the most basic information. The only communication the majority of us have with our local police is through the large, yellow boards set up on pavements after a serious crime. Apart from an appeal for witnesses, these tell us the nature of the crime and when it happened. We never hear the follow-up. We never learn whether the culprits have been arrested, gone to court and received a sentence.

I contacted my police station to find out what crime happened where in my neighbourhood. It seemed a simple question. I had told my children to cross a busy road rather than take the underpass—dark, smelling of urine and frequently vandalised. Was I paranoid? How many muggings had actually taken place there? The police had no idea. More to the point they were flummoxed by the question. When Safer Neighbourhood Policing began, I asked the constable if we could receive a monthly crime report by e-mail. My question left him dumbfounded. It was, he said, out of the question.

It is not in the USA. There police issue weekly lists of all reported crime. Crime victims know their crime has been recorded. Neighbours are alerted and can protect themselves, and residents can judge for themselves whether crime is high or not in their area. Most importantly it allows residents to ask two vital questions. How are their local police responding? And when they do respond, how is the criminal justice system dealing with the criminals?

When an American asked community liaison officers for something similar here, they refused. A crime list, they insisted, might alarm people. It might indeed. But public ignorance makes it easier for the police and the Crown Prosecution Service to get away with a poor service.

Community policing depends on problem solving, proactive policing. It depends on the police really knowing their neighbourhoods, building trust and acquiring intelligence. How much this was lacking I discovered on a visit to my local shopping street while investigating crime in my neighbourhood in 2004.

The Indian chemist, also the representative of the local traders association, was clear: 'We are very concerned. Crime is a serious issue for all businesses in the area. Gangs are hitting stores even in broad daylight.'

Every shop had suffered at least one incident in the previous few months. Gangs from the local estate stole a TV from the local pub, smashed open the florist with a garbage bin, smashed the window of the wine shop and helped themselves to goods in the newsagent, the chemist and the supermarket. The chemist went on: 'They are quite aggressive and do it openly'. One man had filled up a trolley. 'I ran after him but he had two friends.'

The shopkeepers tried ringing the police. No one came or came too late. They tried sending their local police station videos of the incidents 'at £3 a shot' said the Lebanese florist. They never heard anything back. 'They get lost in the system', said the chemist, 'The police don't think it's worth the bother.' The police told the shopkeepers they were too busy fighting major crime.

That was a pity. They might have learnt something if they had joined the owner of the local deli for a cup of coffee in the café next door. Safer Neighbourhood Policing is also about gathering intelligence. Sid, the deli owner, claimed a gang was using the café as their headquarters from which to deal drugs, organise prostitutes and distribute fake documents. A group of men in gold chains and speaking Arabic had monopolised the two best window tables. Each had two mobile phones into which they talked constantly. Occasionally one walked over to the white van parked opposite and conferred with a young, good-looking man in a Versace T-shirt. Sid claimed he saw about 12 different men during the day driving girls around, delivering drugs 'and once I saw a big bag of fake passports falling out of the van'. The café owner had tried to get rid of the gang but 'was too scared' to do much.

There seemed an extraordinary level of criminal activity in such a small shopping street. Where were the police? Sid shrugged: 'The local police are never here. It is not seen as a crime hot spot.' A policeman might sometimes patrol, 'but it is always a different one'. We watched a warden ticket the white van. 'If only the police were as effective', said Sid gloomily.[3]

One retired member of Special Branch pointed out that: 'Policing is a people's business'. Getting to know your neighbourhood is nothing new. When he started, in order to pick up local intelligence: 'your sergeant encouraged you to have a tea-hole'. A good tea-hole belonged to someone who because of their job, lifestyle or just natural curiosity and sociability knew what was going on. It could be in the back of a shop, a café such as in my shopping street or the front room of an inquisitive old lady. As a probationer he was sitting in a popular tea-hole—the back of a pub with his sergeant having a beer—when two burglars broke in, 'So we nicked them. No one asked what were we doing there.'

On a walk around my local estate with two PCSOs, we paused in front of some lock-up garages. The two women stop there regularly. As Sir Ian Blair pointed out, Safer Neighbourhood Policing is vital to both serious crime and terrorism. It is neighbourhood police who pick up early clues. Who is buying suspicious amounts of peroxide? Why is there an unusual number of comings and goings at a certain flat or lock-up garage? Or who is selling fake passports from the local café?

One member of the serious crime squad agreed. 'People in the community know where you go to get finance, drugs or guns. They just lack the bigger picture.' He had spent nine months building a case against two brothers. They dealt in coke, enforced debt and supplied guns. They lived on an estate of mainly professionals, 'but everyone knew they were into organised crime'. They were 'a real pain in the neck' and it got them talked about. They assaulted the local Pakistani mini cab drivers, slapped women around and picked fights in the local pubs. When the brothers were sentenced, the police added an e-mail address to the story in the local press for people to respond. They received 80 e-mails from the community thanking them. 'So that made it worthwhile', remarked the detective.

A detective in a murder squad said he would never begin house-to-house enquiries after a murder until he had discussed it with the neighbourhood team. Residents 'wont talk unless you have got neighbourhood police building blocks in place', he explained.

Safer Neighbourhood Policing is popular with the public. In July 2003 an ICM poll for the think-tank, Reform questioned public support for zero tolerance— highly visible policing on the streets bearing down heavily on anti-social behaviour and vandalism. Eighty-three per cent thought this to be a good idea.

Over half thought it a very good idea. Older voters were the keenest on zero-tolerance policing. Young voters were only marginally less keen. Seventy-seven per cent of 18- to 24-year-olds supported it. Eighty-seven per cent of Conservative voters and 85 per cent of Labour voters were enthusiastic, while the strongest support came from C2 and DE classes—the least economically advantaged groups. Since the start of Safer Neighbourhood Policing, the shopkeepers in my area report a definite drop in crime.

Safer Neighbourhood Policing also appeared popular with many police officers. They were excited to discover that creative thinking and council support could make a difference. One response officer had transformed a large open space previously notable for muggings and drug-taking. He got the council to install light bulbs, 'which lit up the whole area' and made a couple of 'lucky arrests'. Residents began to walk their dogs there. They would stop and chat to him.

Safer Neighbourhood Policing needs a radically different approach to that of the 'sausage machine mentality of senior management'. An officer looked at the incidents of robbery in his area. He had a choice: 'We can patrol at 10 p.m. and nick the robbers.' Instead he tried to work out why the offences were happening. 'Then', as he explained, 'take it back then back again until you deal with the root cause of the problem.' He discovered a number of problem families had been housed in the same area: 'So they have a bit of an empire. They have a bit of status.' He asked the council

63

to get those families dispersed and put an end to the robberies.

However there are concerns. The government plans to provide the extra police needed for Safer Neighbourhood Policing by reducing bureaucracy and thus freeing up 12,000 officers. But bureaucracy has not fallen. Home Officers figures show that officers spend almost 20 per cent of their time on paper work in the station and just 14 per cent out on patrol. 'Instead of getting on with the job', as one pointed out, 'you are chained in front of the computer monster you have to feed.' Another recalled: 'When I joined the police you needed three pieces of paper to prosecute anyone. Now it's a minor rainforest.'

A lack of officers is part of a bigger problem. Despite both public and police enthusiasm, government commitment appears to be faltering. Forces have relied heavily on the recruitment of PCSOs to develop Safer Neighbourhood Policing. In November the government went back on its manifesto pledge to recruit 24,000 PCSOs by 2008. It has reduced the target to 16,000. At the same time it removed £70 million of funding for Safer Neighbourhood Policing. The government claimed this was in answer to police requests for flexibility. As the President of ACPO, Ken Jones, commented in a letter to chief constables: 'Being given the flexibility to manage decline is not a position we have sought.'[4]

The government knows full well the importance of numbers to make its policy a success. *Building Safer Communities Together* states: 'It is important that forces have sufficient capacity in terms of resources to ensure that neighbourhood officers are not regularly taken away from their areas to perform other duties.'[5]

In London the Met has police officers dedicated to safer neighbourhood teams in addition to response teams. Few other forces enjoy that luxury. Despite government policy, they are forced to rely on police performing a joint role as both response and neighbourhood officers. ACPO recently published figures revealing that less than ten per cent of officers in England and Wales are dedicated to Safer Neighbourhood Policing.

Police at every level described the tensions between response and community policing when both are competing for limited resources.

A response officer summed up the dilemma: 'Our main role is law and order'. When resources are in dispute, 'you can't be all pink and fluffy as well'.

Initially officers moved from response to neighbourhood teams. But response, as we have seen, is perilously short staffed. In order to get calls answered, police from neighbourhood teams found themselves hijacked or rather, as they lack cars, made to walk to incidents.

A number of neighbourhood police complained, for example, that their shift pattern had changed. This was not to improve how they policed the neighbourhood but to help response over their busiest period—late duty on a Friday and Saturday night. But, as one pointed out, 'a rigid half-night shift system' is not always compatible with local policing. How, said one sergeant, could he arrange a meeting with a local councillor at 8 p.m. on a Friday evening? Or visit residents who had left messages for him at two in the morning?

Another sergeant summed up the disillusionment of many. He had invited the public along to an open meeting. He had told them that the police 'and our partners on this panel want to address your issues'. He had asked residents to list their concerns then vote on them. He promised that 'we will take away three of those issues, look at them and report back to you next month'. Then along came the new shift system. He and his colleagues complained to senior officers that it would 'impact severely', but to no avail. Covering response sergeants took precedence over community policing. He explained: 'We are not doing our job properly because we're used as a secondary resource to response.' This jeopardised the project and his relationship with the public. 'So we're setting ourselves up for a fall straightaway.'

Making a commitment then failing to resource it properly is causing bitterness and disillusionment amongst both the public and the police. One young officer described his experience. He found himself a neighbourhood police officer in a rough area. 'I loved it.' The locals complained about a youth club. He was reluctant to close down the only one in the area—'where would the kids go?' He discovered the club was short-staffed and had an age limit of 21. It was the older youths who were causing the problems. First he successfully argued for a younger cut-off age. Then he and a member of the council visited the youths at home together. They explained bad behaviour would no longer be tolerated. They warned the families they might lose their council flats. 'Well they wouldn't but they didn't know that.'

He had to patrol a large area so he introduced a police station in the form of a cabin. This proved a great success. 'People loved it.' He also involved the kids who hung around causing trouble in sponsored car washes. He had worked for two years in the neighbourhood. 'By putting time and effort into it, it's been a real success. It's been really good.'

But all that had changed. Instead of concentrating on his Safer Neighbourhood Policing, he now had to do response work as well. 'It's come full circle. It's gone back to being what it was before.' At any time the radio can summon him away. It was not just the emergency calls either. He had follow-up investigations. He was working on a case of credit card fraud. This meant he spent most of the time out of his area. As for the cabin that had proved so popular, the force had sold it. 'They can't have made much from it and the public responded that well.' The previous weekend 200 youths had a mass fight on his patch. 'One lad had a golf club to his head—and that's all down to us no longer patrolling the streets.' He was so disillusioned he had decided to leave the force. 'It's pathetic isn't it? You can't make it up.'

As well as failing to follow through on its commitment to Safer Neighbourhood Policing, the government also refuses to accept the logical outcome of involving the public in policing. More concentration on local issues must mean less control from the centre. More involvement of the public must mean that they, rather than the Home Office, will direct and judge the police. But at this the Home Office baulks. Consulting the public is fine. Allowing them to decide how they want to be policed is apparently not. Officers find themselves pulled in two directions and it's the Home Officer that is winning out.

Forces are still judged by the all important sanctioned detections rather than how well they are implementing Safer Neighbourhood Policing. This means that power is firmly with the centre and not the community. A borough commander explained his dilemma. He has to keep up his level of sanctioned detections. At the same time his officers are working hard to befriend their local communities. This was paying dividends in less crime being committed. However their success did not help the borough commander. 'There are some wards', he said gloomily, 'where my men are doing such a marvellous job that they are not arresting anyone. And I simply cannot afford to have 150 policemen making no arrests.'

Borough Commanders need to enjoy greater control of their budgets if they are going to improve policing locally. But here again the centre is reluctant to let go. One commander illustrated his lack of autonomy. He asked his force if he could give up a couple of response cars in exchange for the money equivalent in bicycles. He was told this was not possible. As he said: 'I'm in charge of 750 cops, but I can't trade in a car for ten or so bikes'.[6]

This appeared true at every level of the force. One inspector said: 'Your whole reputation stands and falls on figures not... how well you're doing with the community.' He pointed out that his community wanted something done about youth crime. 'They see that as a priority [but] the powers that be don't and that's the difference.' Another inspector agreed. The public want the police to deal with anti-social issues. 'But it doesn't really create any great sort of measure for the division because we don't get measured on that.'

A sergeant had been asked to do something about drug dealing at his last PACT meeting (Partners and Communities Together). 'So I vowed to solve the problem.' In the first two weeks he issued 12 warrants against the dealers in the area. This had great impact. The dealers moved off and residents were delighted.

Then suddenly his division refused to sign any more warrants. They gave two reasons, neither of which had anything to with giving the public the policing they wanted. The division had 'hit greens in drugs'. In other words it had reached its target so drugs were no longer a priority. Then the warrants— although effective against drug dealers—did not earn sanctioned detections for his chief superintendent. The sergeant continued: 'I've been handcuffed by management because its not performance-indicated for them.'

So angry was the sergeant that he had primed 'one of my residents' to ask at the next public meeting how many warrants were being issued. 'And I will say what's going on in front of the press', said the sergeant, 'And I won't tell lies—but I will be kicked by the chief superintendent.'

Officers interviewed feared that finite resources and conflicting targets meant that Safer Neighbourhood Policing has to fail. A Borough Commander admitted: 'I am scared it's going to be watered down.' A district inspector pointed out that Safer Neighbourhood Policing had initially been well resourced in his area but the latest round of cuts had left him gloomy. 'I think we have conned the public.'

Conclusion

How the Good Guys Can Win

Just before Christmas a retired police officer was withdrawing money from an ATM machine when he noticed a small monitoring device attached to it. He pulled off the device and telephoned the police. He rang four times in 38 minutes. Finally he told the call centre he could not wait any longer; unless they turned up in the next few minutes he would stamp on it. 'Well, I don't think I am being well served', he remarked, 'and they knew I was a police officer!'

The police are no longer sure what their role is. Is it to solve a murder or sort out disputes in the playground? Is it to fulfil government targets, fix an old lady's central heating or, as one officer was recently told, to get the overhanging bushes in his area cut back. Piecemeal reform has left the police subject to conflicting demands. Sanctioned detections versus professional integrity; the demands of the centre versus the needs of the local community: all these and more hobble our police service. 'I am not a social worker', said one police officer emphatically. 'I never trained as a social worker. I am paid to catch the baddies and whack them in front of the courts.' He pointed out that Italy and France enjoy a two-tiered system. They have a local force for local issues and a national force for serious crime. 'We suffer from a lack of clarity of role', he said.

Simon Reed, Bedfordshire Officer and member of the National Committee of the Police Federation, wants to see targets replaced by a few big outcomes such as service delivery and a reduction in crime and anti-social behaviour. He explained: 'The outcomes should be set, not by the Home Office, but local borough commanders in consultation with their communities.' Keith Hunter, a former Commander of the Met, pointed out that most of the 'dynamism' in policing in recent years has occurred in 'forward-looking, autonomous American police departments, subject to greater democratic control'.[1]

In other words, the government must get out of the job of policing. Targets divert the police from long-term solutions. The politicisation of the force emphasises the quick fix. Police are at the mercy of politicians desiring major reform but not around long enough to pursue the incremental changes such reform requires. As in the NHS, constant reform has resulted in confusion and inconsistency. 'Chaotic', 'crazy', 'unreal' and 'barking mad' were the reactions of officers faced with 'yet another initiative'.[2]

The result is the very opposite of that 'dynamism' envisaged by Keith Hunter. As one chief constable said bitterly: 'We are measured month by month. It absolutely encourages short-termism.' Central control means that for the police, as for the NHS: 'People of vision are not at liberty to implement that vision'. This was said by a senior non-executive director of an NHS hospital but her experience echoes that of Safer Neighbourhood Policing officers. Another new initiative is always on its way 'to give you a bloody big sweep off your chosen road'.[3]

At the heart of our disjointed police service is the attitude of the government and the Home Office. It is very simple. They do not believe that crime is a problem and a policeman on every corner the answer. Jacqui Smith, Home Secretary, told parliament in December 2007 that the 2006/07 crime survey shows that, since peaking in 1995, 'crime has fallen by 42 per cent representing eight million fewer crimes'. Home Office publications repeat that crime is 'historically low' and the real problem is the public's irrational 'fear of crime'. A senior police office contended: 'The root cause of the problem is that fear of crime is totally out of kilter with crime itself.' This is what Sir Ian Blair described as 'a success gap'—that is, a gap between, 'what we say we are delivering and what the public think we are delivering'.

Is the public behaving irrationally? A recent Home Office survey revealed that half of us believe crime in our area actually increased in the last two years. But then crime is not low compared to the past. In 1972 there were 8,900 robberies in the whole of England and Wales. In 2001/2 there were 6,500 in the London Borough of Lambeth alone. Home Office reports like to put down fear of crime to newspaper readership, but again it is not quite as irrational as the Home Office makes out. Between 1999 and 2003 the tabloid readers of Lambeth suffered 18,565 robberies. The *Guardian*-reading Home Office official in Richmond, however, put up with just 1,040. Or as a CPS solicitor remarked to group of incredulous police sergeants: 'Well of course I take disorder on our streets seriously. I have seen it on my TV. It looks awful.'

As with immigration and the NHS, good, independent data is hard to come by. Home Office statisticians and the Office for National Statistics lack autonomy. Many if not all statistical reports are still being submitted to ministers for approval of their content and the times of their release. Then the actual number of crimes that take place is anybody's guess. In 2001 for example, depending on whether you prefer police figures, the British Crime Survey or various Home Office research studies, the figure ranged from 13 million to 60 million crimes. The British Crime Survey, described by the Home Office as 'the most reliable measure of crime', does not include crimes against anyone under the age of 16. The same lack of data extends to those under 16 who commit crimes. Youth crime particularly concerns the public. Yet it took a Freedom of Information request to each of the 43 police forces to uncover that four out of ten muggings are committed by children under 16—and that is only the ones reported.

It is hardly surprising, therefore, that the public remain sceptical of crime statistics—especially when they can not get even the most basic information on crime in their local area. Peter Fahy, chief constable of Cheshire, warned top officers against claiming crime is falling when the public see only 'disorder and lack of control'. He went on: 'If you tell them things are better, you destroy your own credibility and their trust in you.'

Take one local authority's attempt to get the message across. They offered prizes to the residents who guessed the correct number of house burglaries committed per week in their area. The residents guessed an average of 202 incidents a week. The actual figure was 27. A Safer Neighbourhood Policing sergeant said: 'People are more scared than they should be of crime. A lot of work hangs around public perception.'

Yet what conclusion is the public expected to draw? Try reporting a burglary of your home. How many hours—even days—does it take before you get a visit from the police? In London, unless the burglar is actually in your house, they refuse to send a car. Whether crime is 'historically low' or the public misinformed does not matter. The police behave as if they are overwhelmed. So that is how we feel about crime too.

The public clearly want more police on the beat. Yet here too the Home Office is ambivalent. A top officer summed up the attitude. 'Hundreds of police standing on every street corner is not the best use of public money. In the long term it does not stop crime.' He added: 'We are so focused on reducing crime that we don't have the officers to patrol.' This view dates from the 1970s and 1980s when the Home Office and academia believed that foot patrols and the police in general could do little to prevent crime.

One leading expert in the USA even began his book on policing with a chapter entitled 'The Myth of the Police' which argued: 'The police do not prevent crime.

Experts know it, the police know it but the public does not know it.'[4]

Bill Bratton, the legendary police chief who turned around five police institutions, proved this fatalistic attitude wrong. He dramatically reduced New York's crime figures by, amongst other reforms, putting more police on the beat. Between 1994 and 1996 felony crime fell by 39 per cent, murders by 50 per cent and theft by 35 per cent. Polls report that public confidence in the NYPD soared from 37 per cent to 73 per cent.

Coupled with this view on policing is the Home Office's equally pessimistic belief that prison does not work. So we have more and more criminals serving their sentences in the community. The Home Secretary recently announced that only those with sentences longer than a year would go to prison. This view is at direct odds with the experience of the police. Police officers, as one pointed out, view prison as the solution, 'because dramatic effects can be seen almost immediately'. Crime drops in the offender's neighbourhood 'and the longer the prison sentence, the longer the drop in crime'. Quality of life improves because prolific criminals 'seek their thrills not just by taking drugs but by assaulting people, joyriding in cars and turning their neighbourhoods into jungles'. A Safer Neighbourhood Policing sergeant explained why crime had fallen in my area. He had ten repeat offenders responsible for the majority of incidents. Eight of the ten were in jail. 'But they will be back on the streets in a few months,' he said cheerfully, 'and all hell will break out'.

Against this background of official scepticism, it is easy to understand why Safer Neighbourhood Policing is 'conning the public'. It is there, as we are constantly told, for 'reassurance'. But a renewed or restored confidence is not the same as the sea change in policing that both the public and the police were led to expect. Reassurance without resources smacks of the publicity stunt.

At the moment local taxpayers lack any power to question ever higher policing costs. They have no say on the number of police walking their neighbourhood. They are unable to insist on even the basics of good service. When they report a crime, does an officer come round, take action then report back? A local tax to pay for the Basic Command Unit and a BCU commander who is selected and answerable to taxpayers whether through local government or even direct elections would give the public that power. It would revive interest in local democracy. Safer Neighbourhood Policing has shown how effectively the police and local councils can work together to combat anti-social and criminal behaviour. The next step is to build on this success and give it substance with local funding and accountability. Sadly the government seems more interested in playing footsy with the electorate than in taking that step.

Where does that leave the police? At the end of his Dimbleby Lecture in 1973, the former Commissioner of the Metropolitan Police, Sir Robert Mark, pointed out that we enjoy a unique style of policing that we should not take for granted. 'If we in Great Britain are to continue to police by consent... we must avoid a drift to alienation of police and people.'[5] At an interview a group of response officers were riffling through the latest government initiatives. One banged the pile of papers, 'There is no quality here whatsoever', he exclaimed. 'But in this room, looking around, you have got quality people and they are being abused.'

Appendix

The following set of principles, which lay out in the clearest and most succinct terms the philosophy of policing by consent, appeared as an appendix to *A New Study of Police History* by Charles Reith (London: Oliver and Boyd, 1956). Reith was a lifelong historian of the police force in Britain, and this book covers the early years of the Metropolitan Police following the passage of Sir Robert Peel's 'Bill for Improving the Police in and near the Metropolis' on 19 June 1829. Reith notes that there are particular problems involved in writing police history, owing to the loss or destruction of much early archive material, and, probably for this reason, the principles appear without details of author or date. However, it seems most likely that they were composed by Charles Rowan and Richard Mayne, as the first and joint Commissioners of the Metropolitan Police. Rowan was a military man and Mayne, 14 years his junior, a barrister. Rowan retired in 1850 leaving Mayne as sole Commissioner until his death in 1868. The sentiments expressed in the 'Nine Principles' reflect those contained in the 'General Instructions', first published in 1829, which were issued to every member of the Metropolitan Police, especially the emphasis on prevention of crime as the most important duty of the police. Reith notes that Rowan and Mayne's conception of a police force was 'unique in history and throughout the world because it derived not from fear but almost exclusively from public co-operation with the police, induced by them designedly by behaviour which secures and maintains for them the approval, respect and affection of the public' (p. 140).

The Nine Principles of Policing

1. To prevent crime and disorder, as an alternative to their repression by military force and severity of legal punishment.

2. To recognise always that the power of the police to fulfil their functions and duties is dependent on public approval of their existence, actions and behaviour and on their ability to secure and maintain public respect.

3. To recognise always that to secure and maintain the respect and approval of the public means also the securing of the willing co-operation of the public in the task of securing observance of laws.

4. To recognise always that the extent to which the co-operation of the public can be secured diminishes proportionately the necessity of the use of physical force and compulsion for achieving police objectives.

5. To seek and preserve public favour, not by pandering to public opinion; but by constantly demonstrating absolutely impartial service to law, in complete independence of policy, and without regard to the justice or injustice of the substance of individual laws, by ready offering of individual service and friendship to all members of the public without regard to their wealth or social standing,

by ready exercise of courtesy and friendly good humour; and by ready offering of individual sacrifice in protecting and preserving life.

6. To use physical force only when the exercise of persuasion, advice and warning is found to be insufficient to obtain public co-operation to an extent necessary to secure observance of law or to restore order, and to use only the minimum degree of physical force which is necessary on any particular occasion for achieving a police objective.

7. To maintain at all times a relationship with the public that gives reality to the historic tradition that the police are the public and that the public are the police, the police being only members of the public who are paid to give full-time attention to duties which are incumbent on every citizen in the interests of community welfare and existence.

8. To recognise always the need for strict adherence to police-executive functions, and to refrain from even seeming to usurp the powers of the judiciary of avenging individuals or the State, and of authoritatively judging guilt and punishing the guilty.

9. To recognise always that the test of police efficiency is the absence of crime and disorder, and not the visible evidence of police action in dealing with them.

Notes

Introduction: Why Can't We Get the Policing We Want?

1   *Daily Telegraph*, 23 January 2008, p. 21.

2   Loveday, B. and Reid, A., *Going Local: Who should run Britain's Police?* London: Policy Exchange, 2003, p. 33.

3   Sergeant, H., *Managing Not to Manage: Management in the NHS*, London: Centre For Policy Studies, 2003, p. 9.

4   Table on Public Policing Preferences from Fitzgerald *et al*, 2002:41, quoted in Loveday and Reid, *Going Local*, 2003, p. 15.

5   Loveday and Reid, *Going Local*, 2003, p. 33.

1: Why Has the Public Lost Faith in the Police?

1   Ipsos Mori quoted in *The Economist*, 26 January 2008, p. 39.

2   Ministry of Justice, *The Economist*, 26 January 2008, p. 39.

3   Sergeant, H., 'Paying Twice' *Civitas Review*, Vol. 1, issue 4, December 2004.

4   Quoted in Herbert, N. *et al*., 'Policing for the People', interim report of the Police Reform Taskforce, 2007.

5   *Statistics England and Wales 2006/07*, London: IPCC (Independent Police Complaints Commission).

6   *Daily Telegraph*, 15 November 2007.

2: Who Responds to Crime?

1   *Daily Telegraph*, 2 April 2007.

2   The European Sourcebook of Crime and Criminal Justice Studies quoted in Herbert, N. *et al*., 'Policing for the People' Interim report of the Police Reform Taskforce, 2007.

3   Dennis, N. and Erdos, G., *Cultures and Crimes: Policing in Four Nations*, London: Civitas, 2005, p. 31.

4   Dennis and Erdos, *Cultures and Crimes*, 2005, p. 79.

5   *Sunday Telegraph*, 4 December 2006.

3: Problems with the Crown Prosecution Service

1   Dennis, N. and Erdos, G., *Cultures and Crimes: Policing in Four Nations*, London: Civitas, 2005.

2   *Daily Mail*, 30 November 2007.

3   Jansson, K. *et al*, Attitudes, perceptions and risks of crime: Supplementary Volume 1 to Crime in England and Wales 2006/07.

4   ICM survey commissioned by the Taxpayer's Alliance, Daily Telegraph, 2 April 2007.

5   *Daily Mail*, 11 December 2007.

6   *Guardian*, 15 January 2008.

7   *Guardian*, 20 August 2007.

8   *Garden Square News*, Vol. 10, Issue 1, Spring 2005.

4: When Targets Distort Policing: Sanctioned Detections

1   Loveday, B., McClory, J. and Lockhart, G. (ed.), *Fitting the Bill: Local Policing for the 21st Century*, London: Policy Exchange, 2007.

2   Loveday, McClory and Lockhart, *Fitting the Bill*, 2007, p. 18.

3   Loveday, McClory and Lockhart, *Fitting the Bill*, 2007, p. 18.

4   *Daily Telegraph*, 21 November 2007.

5   *Sunday Telegraph*, 20 January 2008.

6   *Guardian*, 20 August 2007.

5: Does Safer Neighbourhood Policing Help?

1   Quoted in Herbert, N. *et al.*, 'Policing for the People', interim report of the Police Reform Taskforce, 2007.

2   *Daily Telegraph*, 2 April 2007.

3   Sergeant, H., 'Paying Twice' *Civitas Review,* Vol. 1, issue 4, December 2004.

4   Quoted in Herbert *et al.*, 'Policing for the People', 2007.

5   *Policing: Building Safer Communities Together*, p. 14 quoted in Chatterton, M. and Bingham, E., *24/7 Response Policing in the Modern Police Organisation: A view from the Beat*, January 2006, p. 108.

6   Loveday, B., McClory, J. and Lockhart, G. (ed.), *Fitting the Bill: Local Policing for the 21st Century*, London: Policy Exchange, 2007, p. 22.

Conclusion: How the Good Guys Can Win

1   *The Times*, 7 January 2008.

2   Chatterton, M. and Bingham, E., *24/7 Response Policing in the Modern Police Organisation: A view from the Beat*, January 2006.

3   Sergeant, H., *Managing Not to Manage: Management in the NHS*, London: Centre For Policy Studies, 2003.

4   Quoted in Herbert, N. *et al.*, 'Policing for the People', interim report of the Police Reform Taskforce, 2007.

5   Quoted in Herbert *et al.*, 'Policing for the People', 2007.